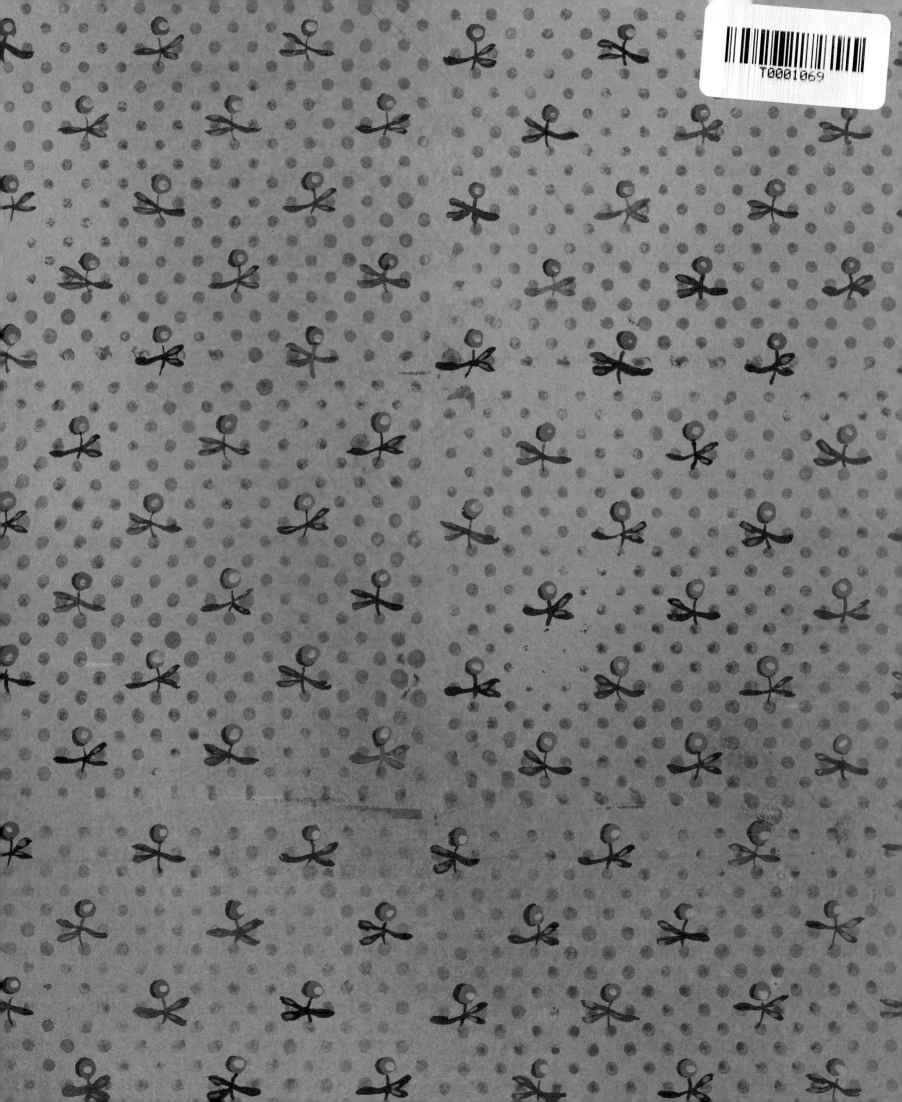

For Bill, who drove the many miles
so that I might see —B.K.

To Elise and Emily —A.J.B.

With thanks to my husband, the artist William Sulit; Michael Hurd and Denise Dorn of the Hurd La Rinconada Gallery; my agent, Karen Grencik; the entire Cameron Kids team; and, of course, Amy June Bates, whose illustrations for this book are so beautiful that I still cry when I see them.

Finally, for their enormous good-heartedness and for the time they spent helping to clarify facts and finalize permissions, I thank Mary Cronin, dean of education & public programs of Brandywine River Museum of Art; Karen Baumgartner of the Museum's Andrew Wyeth Office; and Rebecca Moore, director of Somerville Manning Gallery, who, together with Frank E. Fowler, said yes when we asked if we could include the beautiful still life you see in the back of the book.

Text copyright © 2021 Beth Kephart
Illustration copyright © 2021 Amy June Bates
Book design by Melissa Nelson Greenberg

Library of Congress Cataloging-in-Publication Data available.

ISBN: 978-1-951836-04-7

Printed in China

10 9 8 7 6 5 4 3 2 1

Cameron Kids is an imprint of Cameron + Company

Cameron + Company
Petaluma, California
www.cameronbooks.com

And I Paint It

HENRIETTE WYETH'S WORLD

by Beth Kephart • illustrated by Amy June Bates

cameron kids

Wherever in our world
we want to go, we go—
Pa and me.

To the slosh of the creek.
To the blackberry vine.
To the garden of red and yellow wings.
To the up and down of our battleground,

and the edge over edge of our sky.

"Awaken into your dreams," Pa says,
and I think of the girl I am and the girl I'll be:
A painter, like Pa.
An actress (maybe).
A fairy with wings.

"Shhhh," Pa says, because Carolyn
is in the henhouse, clucking,
not talking to Pa
　　　finally,
not talking to me.

"Shhhh," he says, and we are down the hill now,
away from the henhouse, away from Nat,
who is at his workbench, building
another ship to sail,
another boat to float.

Pa is courteous to the blossom blooms,
and the dirt-road blooms,
and the blooms of thunderclouds.

His big hand is red-and-blue-and-purple freckled,
his old coat smells like apple cores and packing
moss and turpentine.

"Love the object for its own sake, Henriette," Pa says,
only to me,
pointing to the flower,
fine and lucky on its stem,
a fringe for the field.

It's just us, our world, and we paint it.

We paint the nuts in the roots of the trees.
We paint the puff of a train over the clatter of a track,
the green growing into the cap of a strawberry,

and the bright zipper of the blackbirds.

And all this time,
Carolyn and Nat are
overhead and far away and close.
All this time,
Ann is at the piano playing,
and Andy, the newest of the five of us,
is finally
        finally
sleeping.

So that it's only Pa and it's only me,
sensing deeply, like Pa says.
Looking. Seeing. Smelling the air
and the earth,
and the turpentine,
and also that flower.

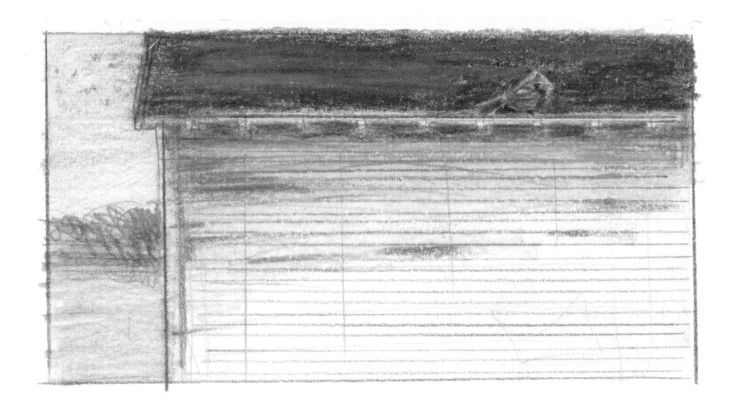

Our world is never still, our world is
falling risking coming drifting flapping.
Our world is a single red bird on the roof of a white farmhouse,

the leap of a frog into the splash of the slosh
of the creek, where the weeping willows
are washing their fairy hair,

and the blue in the sky that is running pink.
"Look," Pa says,

and we paint it.

Pa and I paint until Carolyn's hen escapes.

Pa and I paint until Nat's new
boat shines.

Pa and I paint until Ann's hands grow
tired with their song.

Pa and I paint until Andy is awake.
And now Andy is
         really
awake.
"It's time," Pa says,
"to head on home."

But I say no.
I watch him go.

I stay where I am inside
the basin of our world,
then make my way farther
to my favorite secret hiding place,
where the turtle shell I found last week
is precisely where I left it,
in the artifice of blue light.
The shell is my shell.
The sky is my sky.
The dream is my dream.

And I paint it.

About the story

Henriette Wyeth Hurd, daughter of the famous illustrator N.C. Wyeth, grew up to be a painter, too. Paintings she called *Dusty Butterfly*, *Fire Bird Suite*, *Fantasy*, and *Adolescence*. Paintings of famous people (like movie stars and a president's wife). Paintings of still lifes (a wooden dove, a pumpkin, her favorite flowers), of her family, and of the things that went on inside her dancing imagination. Paintings of her childhood home, in Chadds Ford, Pennsylvania, and paintings of San Patricio, New Mexico, where she lived on a gorgeous ranch with her husband, the painter Peter Hurd, and their children, Peter Jr., Carol, and Michael.

I first found Henriette in her father's proud letters. She was born in 1907, on N.C. Wyeth's birthday; she would always be extraordinarily special to him. "Henriette is astounding in her powers of perception and her sense of logical reasoning," he wrote. He wrote about her sense of humor and her independent streak. He wrote about sitting with her in his grand studio painting, or taking her out into the world to show her the clouds, the birds, the secret history of the land where they lived. He wrote, too, about the care she took of her four younger siblings—Carolyn and Andrew (who would also become painters), Ann (who played the piano and composed music before turning to painting, too), and Nat (who became an important engineer).

I fell in love with this Henriette.

I started to read all about her, visit her childhood home, study her paintings, talk to people who collected them. Once I even drove halfway across the country so that I could see her San Patricio ranch, and that is where I met her son, Michael. I got to see some of Henriette's early sketchbooks, read some of the postcards and letters she sent and received, walk around in the home she created, stay on the land itself for a few days, stand inside her painting studio. I even brought home with me, thanks to Michael's generosity, one of Henriette's color palettes. It hangs on the wall behind me as I write this.

In this story, I create an imaginary day in the life of Henriette and her father. The N.C. Wyeth words "Awaken into your dreams" and "Love the object for its own sake" are borrowed from Wyeth's article "For Better Illustration," which originally appeared in *Scribner's Magazine* in November 1919. The term "the artifice of blue light" is a term Henriette herself used; in fact, it was the title of one of her monographs. —B.K.

Floral Still Life, by Henriette Wyeth
© Henriette Wyeth. Image courtesy of Somerville Manning Gallery and Frank E. Fowler

About the illustrations

I come from a family of artists. I was taught drawing from my dad and painting from my uncle. I spent summers painting outdoors, up the canyon with my grandma and hiking through the mountains with my grandpa, always running to catch up with him. Now with kids of my own, I love painting and exploring the outdoors with them. I teach them to pay attention to the clouds and the specific color at the center of a flower or the character in the gnarled roots of an old tree. But then they return the favor by teaching me to look up and chase a frog or notice a mushroom ring or to put my feet in a cold creek and skip a rock. I became interested in the Wyeths as a thirteen-year-old, just a bit older than Henriette in this book. I loved the magical, fantastic world that their family created in Chadds Ford; I wanted to live in it. For me this book was a combination of past and present, homage and memory, but mostly getting outside and letting nature inspire. —A.J.B.

*"The great and exciting thing
about something beautiful is that it's
almost gone before you realize it.
I have realized beauty and I've been with it."*

—Henriette Wyeth Hurd, *The Artifice of Blue Light.*